A Stranger's Broken Language

- Poems for Timeless Seeker -

Young Jun Kim

Order this book online at www.trafford.com
or email orders@trafford.com

Most Trafford titles are also available at major online book retailers.

Printed in the United States of America.

ISBN: 978-1-4669-4708-5 (sc)
ISBN: 978-1-4669-4709-2 (e)

Trafford rev. 07/20/2012

 www.trafford.com

North America & international
toll-free: 1 888 232 4444 (USA & Canada)
phone: 250 383 6864 ♦ fax: 812 355 4082

To my mother, father and uncle, Ae Sook Park,
Doo Pyo Kim and Han Pyo Kim.
To MeSun Hospice, GCU, Erskine Theological Seminary,
and Atlanta Saints Presbyterian Church

"Who is he that hideth counsel without knowledge? therefore
have I uttered that I understood not; things too wonderful for me,
which I knew not. Hear, I beseech thee, and I will speak:
I will demand of thee, and declare thou unto me."

—Job 42: 3-4

Contents

Preface

Stranger, this is a universal term. I believe it. Nobody can avoid this ontological identity. We are born a stranger, and will pass away someday and somewhere. The reason that I use this phrase is my experience of journey as a stranger. So I would like to choose this term, 'stranger' as a title of my poem. Readers will find that my poems have a brokenness in language. This brokenness is my limitation. So I cannot avoid the term, 'broken language.' But I think ontology is a fundamental issue than language. It takes courage to write poems. How to evoke such a struggle from my feeling as a human being and a spiritual care giver, is my the unceasing question within my poem style. Even though my poems seem like a naïve person's expression, my poems show enigmatic expression as much as brokenness, but I like to be a naïve stranger as naïve means to be a sage in Eastern thought and is spiritual evoking.

Thanks to Trafford; Mee Sook, Isaac, Isaiah, Lee-Lye, and Ee Sl Kim, and also Young Ha Kim who is a devotional professor and minister. Especially thanks to Forum Writers at Barns&Nobles.

Naked Trees

Naked trees
The wisdom of equality
Even if proud of their uniqueness, speechless color
At the fall
They know how to be one with other friends
At the winter

Silent sages
Divine wisdom hides in the naked trees
But we cannot read that wisdom
Due to our blindness

Nature is nature
We see nature as a necessity
The nature of Cain
Selfishness is our nature
So,
To be a naked person
is
Divine nature, as
Nobody avoids nakedness from birth to death.

With One Who is Going to Eternal Time

With one who is going to eternal time is a gap between mysteries of life.
To be a gap being is always challenge.
Due to my ignorance, limited emotion, and
Meaning of abandoning everything.

Normally people say to finish is to start.
It is easy word for emotion.
Even we have several hundred thousand words,
We never explain that word, start.
So we may say symbolically.
This is evidence of our ignorance.
This reason, we try relying on divine being who knows exact word.

Today I gave several words for the one who is going to eternity.
And I said several words for his soul with divine words.
Without knowing dying, just giving comfortable emotion for him.

Ignorance means pretending, at least my feeling.
How can I grasp the maturity?
Unceasing struggle for my vocation
Just I am a person for the symbol.

A Sound of Journey to Eternity

When I said, "Let us pray"
He started his hands together.
He drifted from consciousness
And turned to unconsciousness
Snoring
Is it a sound to eternal journey?

Long time ago
My mother said,
"There is a sound of journey to eternal world. It starts from snoring"
I did not understand mother's saying.
But now I found out.

Did he hear his sound of journey to eternity?
Like a train with whistle
Like a sound of a paddling boat to cross Jordan River
May be, he was crossing Han River to see his friends.

Rue

Rue is a path to mystery.
It is molding me with purity.
But, we are living as if avoiding it.
That is our limitation.

Rue is a path to see the invisible world.
It leads to another recognition.
We rise against it.
That is our blindness.

Rue is a path to bitterness.
Its tastes like an herb, a dandelion root.
That we struggle not to swallow.
Such is our folly.

Life is a paradox.
To avoid rue is our life.
It is an unavoidable reality.
We should be used to it as a path to our own mythology.

When I visit to My Father's Tomb

When I visit to my father's tomb,
I always find that I was such a spoil kid.
Like a prodigal son.
There were several chances in my life,
Among them to honor parents was the first chance,
As a son.
But I never be a good son.
This is my regrettable journey of life.
Now, I am experiencing such a prodigal child.
Now I am passing the huge mountain.

One Reason to be a Good Person

Trying to understand people's life history
is a portion of minister.
To deliver sermon for living people
by dead people's life history at the grave yard
Is very tricky job.
So we have to remain some good story.
This is one reason to be a good person.
At the least for the minister.

Between A Good Man and Bad Man

There is a gap between a good man and bad man.
It is alike between one sheet.
If we have the divine eye sight,
We would understand; we are almost same,
Due to sin.
Isn't it universal truth?

Feeding Ducks

Feeding ducks is so funny.
It reflects my military life.
Whenever I throw a piece of cookie,
They all run to get it first.
It doesn't need any self-respect and self-pride,
Like soldiers who wear same dress.

Feeding ducks make me pleasure.
They give me a moment of escaping.
It turns to be a moment of human being.

Two Worlds

There are two worlds.
Rational world and irrational world
Without any reason someone hits me, I had to accept.
This is irrational world.
This is an old soldier's story.

Usually we are living in the rational world.
Especially civilized land has this world.
But I found more contradicted happening in this land of civilization.
High expectation,
But often low result.
Is this our reality?

To Love Is To Be Naïve One

"To love is to be naïve one."
Very uncomfortable phrase,
And not for those young men,
Because it is very hard to understand to them.

I know this phrase is so ambiguous.
To be naïve means to be an unattractive man.
This is young's emotion.
Very sage way of phrase, "to love is to be naïve one."
The phrase of hidden meaning,
And very empirical

Sanctification

Sanctification is one of purpose of salvation.
To be sanctified means to know how to bear the cross.
Very wide and deep word, but easy word to recognize,
Without to bare the cross, we will not be understood this word,
     'sanctification.'
It is very deep and wide knowledge,
'Sanctification'

There are tremendous people who like to use this word, 'sanctification.'
Word play is today's religion as my notion.
Without practice of God's Word, to be spiritual contentment is
     drunken emotion of the religion.
So reformed preachers may emphasize doing theology.
To be sanctified one and satisfied with doing in faith
Is a huge question to me.

Dried Sky

Even I want to rain,
The sky is still drying.
Blue and no clouds on the sky,
Like eyes of bride who has a first night with bridegroom,
Likewise deep blue

If the sky is ocean,
We would experience of Noah's flood.
So dried sky is one of blessing,
Also, we don't need to get into the gate of Noah's ark.
Dried blue sky is one of my blessings.

Preacher's Struggle

You know, what's a preacher's struggle?
When some church member doesn't listen my sermon,
And he starts against sermon with demonstrational behavior like
Looking for Bible verses or chat with other member of beside,
And watching out to window, or sleeping and yawning . . .
It is a time to experience inner angry.
But preacher has to smile.
Because preacher.
Most disciplined actor than Hollywood movie actor is preacher.
Academic prize should be for the preacher.
Because this kind of battle happens at every Sunday.

When My Mother Takes My Hand toward Buddhist Temple

Long time ago, my mother often went up to Buddhist temple,
The mountain of my village.
Usually she bowed hundred times to the Buddha stature
with begging for her husband, kids, my successful life and family
     being rich.

When my mother took my hand toward the Buddhist temple,
She taught me how to bow, and no play at the Buddhist temple.
But I usually played at the yard without bowing to Buddha.
It was one reason to be disciplined at home.

Time has passed,
Now my mother goes to church.
Because she accepted God than Buddha.
Every morning she prays for my success.
Still she takes my hand as when I was a boy.

Starbucks Coffee

Starbucks coffee is a symbol of Americanism.
Like returning colonialism.
Starbucks is conquering whole world.
Old days was times of Coca-Cola,
But now Starbucks is one of symbol of globe.

I am not sure,
Starbucks will be like another Roman empire with chasing people's
        taste,
Or Babylonian empire with symbolical dominant Americanism.
But certainly they are conquering people's tongue.
Anyhow, Starbucks coffee and broken English
Is my unpleasant reality.

At the Tomb of My Father

Strangely I don't cry at the tomb of my father.
I don't know why.
Is the reason of my father's strong image?
"Boy should not show tear."
It was the instruction of my father's days.
But now there are too many boys who are crying.
As if no more boy's pride as a strong image.

My father usually didn't talk too much.
A day three words was father's image.
Just one single father's proverb remains in my memory.
"Tiger remains his skin, but man remains his name."

Now I talk too much to my kids.
"Read, study, clean up your room, wake up early and so on"
But my kids turned to heavy rocks.
I don't know why I become a person like chatter.
Shame and unwise father, I am.

I am not sure what kind of father's image is scribing in their mind.
But certainty,
In a future,
My kids will not cry at my tomb, also.
I believe that.

Dog's Life

Dog's life is sometimes similar to human's life.
So some people say "my life is like dog's life."

Dog's life, I heard a lot of time.
I don't understand exactly, what it means.

When I went to the ranger school, the ranger trainer poured the
    reservoir water
on soil.

So we have to lick the water. Is this like dog's experience?
No!

It is human's life.
Due to we had covenant at the ranger school.

Just before ranger training
They showed just one time, the ranger exercise.

And they made us like a dog.
…

Real human experience!

Spider's Working

Spider is working on my living room.
Without my permission he is in my living room.
The permission, it is a human's territorial length between.
So we always swallow uncomfortable-ness, each other.

Spider is one of nature.
He may think my living room as a nature.
Under the sofa, he can sleep well.
Edge of window, he doesn't matter for his business.
Even my bath room.

This morning he delivers a good sermon for me.

When I Met Young Day's Church Members

After three decades I met young day's church members.
We all became those persons who have some white hair color.
And we all have several kids who are attending college or high school.
Someone's first question was, "do you remember my name?"
I forgot some names, but they never forgot my name.
May be, they have loved me until now.
"Misunderstanding is free."
It is I.
Anyway, my imagination makes me smile.

Among them, some lady gave me her heart at the time of 20s.
When we walked to turn around together the village 'MacheonDong',
She gave me her heart, but I didn't grasp her.
Still she wants to remember her name, but
I forgot her long time ago.
So, she has questioned two times to recall her name.
Is this difference between man and woman?
Anyway, her name is forgotten in my mind.
Because, because she is tall like, Olive in Popeye.

In the Mosquito Tent

Whenever I enter in the mosquito tent, I am seized by amazing.
Opened dark sky, uncountable stars, moon and huge abyss.
Even God gave us freely this spectacle,
But usually we forget this free.
Due to busy, and seizing with own world.

There is another spectacle in the mosquito tent.
This is dance of bugs around bulb.
Even they try to get in the mosquito tent, they only can do dance.
Dance of emptiness?
Dance of vanity?
Or
Demonstration of alive?
Impossible to read their dancing,

God will know their dance of frenzy.
Due to they are His creatures,
This is only the way to know the wisdom of universe,
I believe it.
To know the relationship between Creator and creature,
Is this the way of reading the universe?
I want to confess this recognition.

Hunting Dog is Eaten after Catching Rabbit

Hunting dog is eaten after catching rabbit.
This is very old Chinese proverb.
This one phrase well demonstrates about human's life.
So, nobody can pride his success.
Because we don't know how we will be eaten by some boss.
Living like walking on fragile ice
Is this man's life?

Usually we have seen those honest men became losers to the evil men.
History has showed us this kind of stories.
So we easily lose what the essence is.
And we turn to be realists.
Doesn't it trap of our life?

There Are Two Mice

There are two mice.
Uncomfortable strangers.
At my yard,
At my wife's plants.
I will throw stone.

My Cucumber Plants

I have planted four cucumber plants.
They are growing well.
Soil never lies, I am learning.

I am seizing with amazing.
Every morning,
Because I pick the cucumbers.

Give and take,
This is my math.
They are very honest girls,

Every night,
I gave them,
My urine.

Let the Dead Bury Their Dead

Among the curious words in the Bible, this is the most curiosity.
"Let the dead bury their dead"
Who is dead one and who is not?
To discern dead one and living one never be a simple knowledge.
The reason is that it is very spiritual knowledge,
And essential knowledge.
If we say those people who are Christians are persons of living
    soul,
They will be blamed as dichotomists.
Very Hellenistic world view.
The knowledge to recognize,
"Man is mortal."
Is a great recognition to whom they have soul.
Jesus word, "Let the dead bury their dead" is a way to go
The knowledge, predestination.

Just a Moment Before Rain

Just a moment before rain,
Everything is very calm.
Just an orchestra sound of bugs
Looks mono tone,
ZZee-----------
SSaa-----------
Often single voice,
Very curious dawn time,
Their chorus will be finished,
After rain.

My Daughter Slept With Holding My Leg

During the night, my daughter holds my leg.
I thought her care for my leg,
As she often care of my foot.
When I found the reason of her holding,
I should give my leg.
Due to her fear over the night,
I have to rent my leg.
Very easy roll of fathering.

Sometimes I Want to Draw My Home Town Road

Sometimes I want to draw my home town road.
Because I have walked a lot of roads in my life, and
Still I am walking on some road.
Very strange thing is that I am walking on
Very strange road.
You know?
The name of the road is Mars Hill.
Now I am living there, and every day I am walking,
The road.
Most curious thing is to walk on the roads which
I never know.
It is like football, which way it will bounce.
This is my life,
And everyone's life, I believe.
Likewise universal bounce, it is human's life.

I have been bounced to this strange road,
As much as Mars hill,
From corner of Seoul to South East some road in America,
Isn't it such a mystery?
Long bouncing,
Sometimes I lost my road, where I should go.
Because I often lose the road,
It would be a journey to find me.
It brings me a desire to draw the road of my home town,
To search my identity and
To find out my way.

Today, I will draw my road of home town.

27

To Be No Soul Man

Usually to be no soul man is a moment of being insulted,
Due to my fault.
But all day long this taste,
Revolving in me,
Like a swirling water.
It never ceases in my soul.
To be no soul man is my journey.

A Day of Thunder

A day of thunder, I had repented.
This day I usually looked for my mother.
For being forgiven.
But now I consider this day as a day of being cautious for internet.
That's it.
Dose my life mingle with mouse's urine?
Anyhow I feel that I became a stinky guy.

When My Wife Calls Me

When my wife calls me,
I start assume the reason of call.
Is this confirming call for love?
I feel she wants to hold me.
Love is a being of woman.
To be recognized is man's safety zone.
Anyway the call brings some confirming,
She is my home.

Easy Way to Understand Each Other

Reason of Asian,
Presupposition is hovering in my life.
Prejudice is moving around me.
Life is a journey to understand the reason of human's selfishness,
Due to protect their boundary,
Sin,
The root of being,
It is easy way to understand each other.

What's the language?

The language is a tool of communication.
And,
House of being,
Behavior of being,
Dance of soul;
Being to being,
Nature to nature,
Feeling to feeling,
Symbol to symbol,
Metaphor to metaphor,
Personality to personality,
Man to God,
God to man,
Man to nature,
God to universe,
Spirituality itself,
And,
Spiritual movement,
Humanity itself,
And,
Human's movement,
A present to recognize Divine Mystery,
Theology,
Exposure of Meta physics, and also
Logical way for physics,
A tool to recognize,
That we are human being,

A Desire of Catching Birds

A desire of catching birds is still my dream.
Very childish and foolish I am.
But the desire is still in me.
Is this my spirituality?
Tiny issue and big question,
When Jesus said,
"Look at the birds of the air; they do not sow or reap or store away
in barns, and yet your heavenly Father feeds them. Are you not
much more valuable than they?"
We know,
God feeds birds, and children of God are more valuable than birds.
But when we see His reigning universe to very tiny thing,
Birds are also the mirror of my spirituality.
Everything, His creatures are my mirrors of my spirituality.

Fireworks

July 4th, the day of fireworks,
Everywhere of night sky,
There are dances of night flowers.
Do the flowers know about the meaning of independence?
I think many people waited for this day just for fun with the fireworks.
It might be fireworks are bigger than the day of independence.
Likewise diminishing essence,
I am also far from the essence.
Knowing the essence is happiness of mine.

Sound of My Footstep

I realized
To hear my footstep is one of blessing.
The reason is,
My footstep is sound of orchestra,
With mixing of those sounds; stones, sand, shoes, bird singing,
 swaying trees, wind, and human voices from long distance.

How long time did I forget my footstep?
It has been a long time.
Because I usually hear my inner voices to reject those sounds of
 quarrelsome souls
Whole night those voices never be ceased in my tedious world.
Accusing of uncountable souls
And justifying my soul
Miserable souls' frenzy—
Only the way to avoid those voices is to give prayer for them
To comfort them for their peace

If I have true ears, I hear heavenly sounds from Creator of our souls.
My footstep, other's footstep, and Lord's footstep
My inner voices, other's inner voices and Lord's gentle whisper

Now I am listening my footstep.
Real sound of natural orchestra;
"Sa-gak, Sa—gak, Saga—k"

Flowers on My Desk

Flowers on my desk
By choice they came to me
From abandoned wedding flowers
Destined to fall
Destined to wither
Today I found several falling leaves on my desk

Humiliation is My Life Journey

Humiliation is my life journey.
It is true blessing from heaven.
Because it is the evidence that I am a human being.
And also I should be broken pieces.
As we feel.
We are irresistible arrogance.

Magnolia

Magnolia,
You are a queen of scent.
And,
You are an elegant lady.
I love you. Because you are a southern beauty.

Magnolia,
You are an invincible lady.
Like a length between blue and black eyes,
How can I reach you?
It is too far as much as Pacific ocean.

Magnolia,
You are true southern beauty.
Because you are splendid dream.
Even I try to give my love,
You always avoid my heart.

Magnolia,
You are southern dream, and
Elegant scent,
You are a symbol of true love.
How can I hold your love in my bosom?

A Voice of Spring

I am hearing your voices of spring
In the soil, worms, dandelions, sky, birds, trees, dogs, ducks and me
Unavoidable sounds from sun shining, hazing, dreaming way and
    stream

Spring is now marching all over the village.
Sound of marching like soldier's foot at the windy day
Sound of cautious woman's bare foot at the day of dazzling

At a Spot of the Station

I am standing at a spot of the station.
Somewhere at the corner of Far East,
There are parallel beauties.
Anyway I am a stranger.

I have been eager to stand at some spot.
Because I want to stand at a spot of station.
Now I feel a moment of free,
A moment of breathing fresh air,

It has been long time I had expected.
To grasp my spot,
Usually standing at some station as a stranger,
It was my dream.

Now I am breathing air, the real air.
It has taken long time, to experience the air.
Standing at some spot.
.
Eternally

Raising Kids

Raising kids are mission impossible.
Unable to sleep with uncountable nights,
Due to kids, who are living the land of Aliens
But here is heavenly present.

When they were born they had their destiny.
Even I never knew what their destiny would be,
As my life, wayward wind
Passing through the wilderness likewise wind blowing,

That is unavoidable their destiny.
They would be a wind somewhere.
Like dandelion seeds,
Only what I can do is prayer.

A Memory of Love

A man has a secret memory.
A memory of love.
This memory requires to be sealed
And also this memory requires abandoning
Due to love never be duel.

Sometimes a memory of love never be exposed to a woman.
Because it is a secret garden.
Or
It should be a secret abyss to a man.

Too much hard burden to a man's life hiding the security
But the memory of love hard to release
To a man
Because it became soul of a man.

One soul still remains at some place.
The other soul remains to a man.
Even three decades has passed,
Still the memory has many stories.

Coffin

Coffin is a paradoxical rectangle.
To stay there we have run with all our strength.
You, coffin is a friend of preachers to deliver a cheap sermon.
Because a preacher have used a sermon in the liturgy book.
Same sermon repeats in the grave yard for past Mr. Kim, Mr. Park,
    Mrs. Lee and Mr. Smith.
Anyway, you are all human's house.
To someone, you are a hotel,
But some, you are an inn.
You are a symbol of capitalism.
Like rich man and Lazarus
Anyway,
You are a timeless dwelling place to all men.
Very universal guy.

Ducks in My House

This is my observation.
Ducks, they are searching for food all day along.
Back and forth in my yard, about 2500 foot size.
Their world is my yard.
Do they think my yard as whole universe?
I don't know.
But they are so busy.
They pant for foods.
Dog's food, worms, abandoned rice, bread, Kim-chi, and some
  duck's food . . .
Sometimes, their behaviors are so similar to some human's life.
Even reflecting my life,
Reflecting my cruelty.
And, make me imagine some POW camp.
And also my military life, long before.
Make them give their all zeal just for one cookie.
Very competitive fiery.
Where is the origin of my tricky?
Unavoidable sinner
Total depravity
Sola Gratia!

Bathing at My Yard

At the hot afternoon,
Bathing at the yard is a great benefit,
Only a few people have this privilege.
Due to accustom to our self-respect

But there is some exceptional case to kids
Because they know how to be nature
How to harmonize with nature
So, they are free.

To be naked is to be shame.
This is our common sense.
For the virtue,
I agree this fact.

After Adam's fall
Apron was Adam's symbol of shame.
But it turned to self-respect.
To create secret garden,
So, we started to use apron.

Even God made for him leather dress,
We had started dressed up with a name of pride.

Living in the War

Living in the war is our ontological struggle.
Because our life itself is war.
Fighting each other is our inner nature.
So we are living to fight.
Is it funny?
To obtain victory, we have to defeat the other one, whoever.
This is our existential limitation, as a human being.
The origin of war is always from our inner nature,
So we call it sin.

No fight means no being.
Very paradoxical contradiction.
But it is true.
In this way we are learning the value of Kingdom of God.
To be free means to be a person who can be winner.
This is a value of earth.

If we know the wisdom how to be a loser than winner,
For those people who want to obtain victory,
We will know what the real freedom is.
To be a loser.
To be a free man.
It is real war.

A Woman Who Never See Her Face to the Mirror

There was a song, 'a woman who never see her face to the mirror.'
When I was young, I could not understand this song's phrase.
But the interpretation always remains to time.
Through tremendous mistakes in my life,
I came to understand this phrase.
Because there were so many times avoiding the mirror to see my
　　face.
Due to my small world,
Due to fullness of myself,
Due to unavoidable arrogance of mine,
Due to . . .

Now I am trying to see my face to the mirror,
As much as my winkle on my face.
But today, I didn't see my face to the mirror.

To Be a Natural person

To be a natural person is most hard to chase.
As you know, pretending became our nature.
To be pretending through education, we
Have lost our nature.
So, we are uncomfortable each other.
Sophistication is our goal to success person.
But it is our mirage.
Because it demands money.

To be like country-likeness is not easy also.
So we experience all the time uncomfortable.
One thing we have to know is that
Life is stage, and we are actors.
Very easy way to understand,
How to be nature.

Barriers

There are tremendous barriers in our planet.
Language, culture, generation, religion, and so on
Someway our life struggles with those tremendous barriers.
So I want to confess that I am living like miracle.
Overcoming some barriers is remaining battle to my life.

Now I am struggling with generation and also language barriers
    with my kids.
To overcome the barriers is losing and earning games.
A kind of experiencing hatching egg,
From this world to world and
From this culture to another culture.
Would it be expended to heaven?
Real epistemology, I think.

Just Before Glorification

It has been several years to visit the lady,
For the spiritual care.
But today I heard her life would be one or three days more.
Do you know the most burden thing that is body?
Usually pain conquers being.
Some case, pain conquers someone's belief.
So, body looks evil, due to pain works with body.
As you know pain never works with soul.
It means old and sick body is of human bondage.
So, taking off the body is last happiness,
Due to free from pain, removing the obstacle for spiritual free,
And experience of glorification.

When I visited her, she was ready to take off her body.
Due to her mouth was opened, and her eyes were almost closed.
I delivered spiritual comfort for her, and the hope of the resurrection.
She responded with "A-Men!"
She was a spiritual woman until her last stage of death.
Just remained glorification.
Someday, she will meet with her resurrected body.
We will be surprised with new body like Adam and Eve.

Soul's Crying

Did you hear soul's crying?
Through wind blowing.
There are tremendous souls whom they died with contradiction,
    regret, unfinished love, and scars . . .
So almost tomb have their reasons of unfair of dead.

When a deep night,
When winds are blowing,
We have to hear their stories.
And we need to be a healer as a wounded healer.

Is this minister's job?
Yes,
So we were called for soul healer.
To be soul healer means to interpret those souls' scars.
Without our scars, we cannot read the soul's crying,
Due to no scars no ears.
In this reason, May God allow tremendous harshness to minister?

Acacia

Acacia,
You are the ordinary flower.
Because, you were very easy to touch.

You were presence of flower in my town with a sweet scent.
This is my reason to love you.
You were a flower of a good and bitter memories

When I was a young,
I ate you, a lot of time
You were tastes of sweet and some bitter of grass,
As my wife who was raised in country like a wild flower

You know,
Love always came with joy and diminishes with sorrow.
This is a lesson of love.
At the time of late May, you withered and had gone sadly
Remaining with painful memory.

Acacia,
You are my teacher, and lovingly girl of mine
But I have to stop my love
Due to my wife who gave me a swear of love.
Is this mystery of love?

Wind and Soul

Wind is from the storehouses of God
Soul is from God's breath
I am living by His breath
This is my daily journey
Oh! Lord
I am praising You with my soul.
Because, I am passing one spot in Your hand.

Today You touched my cheek with Your wind
As You secure my soul.
And You whisper me
"I am your Father!"

Lord!
You are my foundation.
You are my dwelling place.
You are my everlasting God.

Wind is from the storehouses of God
Soul is from God's breath
I am Your breath and wind.

Epilogue

Writing poem is most attractive behavior to me. The reason is the purification of my soul and pursuing essential things. So poetic language to me is imageries, metaphors and symbols.

Still, I have an obligation that I have to remain writing for descendants.

This is the first reason to write these poems, because I am a stranger who doesn't know well the dominant language, English. And as a stranger, I have a desire to send what my emotions, struggles and experiences are as a first generation in America..

Secondly, I want to send my devotional emotions from in my inner being and nature. So my poems express some spiritual struggles and devotions in hidden form like metaphor, symbol and story.

Thirdly, my style of poem is narrative or story. This makes me uncomfortable, because I have tried to express with some hidden form of language from my nature and spiritual sight other than phenomena. I have a prayer to recognize that the universal language is human nature through its voices.

Thanks to all my readers!